MW00896667

"Live as if you were to die tomorrow. Learn as if you were to live forever."

- Oscar Wilde

Copyright © 2016 by relaxation4.me. All rights reserved.

MORE BONUS DESIGNS

For all subscribers of our Newsletter we give away another 10(!) FREE Bonus Relaxing Designs. They are beautiful, relaxing and with Your help they will become a true masterpiece.

Get them here:

http://relaxation4.me/bonus-relaxing-designs

Thank You For Investing Your Precious Time In This Book!

After this book was ordered we've asked our specialists to adjust our letterpress machine based on the Gutenberg's original to create this book especially for You. The smell of fresh printing ink was floating through the air of our entire company. With natural-antimicrobial gloves Your book has been gently taken from our printing press and placed under the most up to date electron microscope. A team of seven book specialists inspected Your book and polished the cover to make sure it was in a flawless condition before mailing. Two Zen masters coming from Tibet recited a protection-sutra before putting Your book into the finest cardboard packaging box that was available in the country. We all had a wonderful candlelight meditation afterwards and the whole team waved "Good-bye!" to your package when it was placed in a long black limousine which directly headed to the post office. There our private relaxation4.me jet was already waiting to take Your package in care and fly it directly to Your lovely home.

We hope You will enjoy this book and have many fun hours with it. In commemoration, we have placed Your picture on our wall as "Customer of the Month." We're all exhausted but can't wait for You to come back to relaxation4.me!

Thank you, thank you, thank you!

Hansi, president, relaxation4.me
the little publisher with the best Grown Up Coloring Books for Stress Relief

www.relaxation4.me

relaxation4.me

Stress is a major issue in the 21th century. Almost everybody in our society is influenced by it. Thinking about how we could contribute our part to make this world better, we stumbled upon Grown Up Coloring Books. Recognizing that really many people love them for forgetting about their stressful daily life, we decided to publish our own versions.

We hope You will love them :)

www.relaxation4.me

About the illustrator

Cheriz "chezerie" Cacha is an illustrator and a graphic designer residing in the city of Davao, in the Philippines. Her experiences in graphics include photo editing, creation of marketing materials graphics, and children's book illustration.

Aside from working with graphics, she also spends her free time practicing on some other traditional mediums, such as watercolor, calligraphy, etc.

Ocean Animals, Underwater Creatures and Sea Life is her second project for relaxation4.me. It is a real pleasure for her to share her art to people who needs some relaxation or people who simply just love coloring.

For A More Beautiful Social Media

We want to improve the appearance of the internet with Your help. Send us Your colored masterpieces at info@relaxation4.me or on our Facebook Page and we will show them the planet.

Don't be shy, inspire others!

www.facebook.com/relaxation4me

www.instagram.com/relaxation4.me

The Coloring Flow

The Coloring Flow will help You relieve stress, become more focused, achieve a sense of serenity, be in a state of timelessness, improve Your hand-eye coordination, boost Your creativity and restore overall.

Find.

Find a nice and comfortable place.

Switch Off.

Switch off disturbing electronical devices.

Color.

Find Your favorite illustration and start to color.

Restore.

Feel stress disappearing, relaxation going through Your body and enjoy the moment.

Repeat.

Pause and repeat whenever You like.

Tips From The Pros

Stay Sharp – To be able to get into tight spaces and edges, always make sure that Your crayons are well-sharpened.

Test It - Never be above of experimenting with colors on a scrap paper. Try them, blend them and see if the result looks like the color You would like to use.

Outside The Lines - Never hesitate to color outside the lines. It's Your art, nobody else's.

Double Layer - Put a sheet of paper under the illustration You are about to color to avoid bleeding through.

Colored Mood - Different colors express and affect different emotions and moods. Colors such as purple, green, blue have a calming effect. You can use them if You want to chill out (literally). Bright colors are for energizing, so choose these colors if You want a little inner lift. Warm colors such as yellow, orange and red are the pepper-uppers. You can try these colors to brighten Your bad mood. Dark colors can also carry relaxing energy and You can use them in order to ratchet down Your overactive mind. Light tint and pastels help soothing the soul and they also communicate softness.

Everyday Recovery - Color every day for at least 15 minutes to have an overall positive and relaxing effect on your life. Not the things we are doing once will change our lives, but the things we are doing regularly.

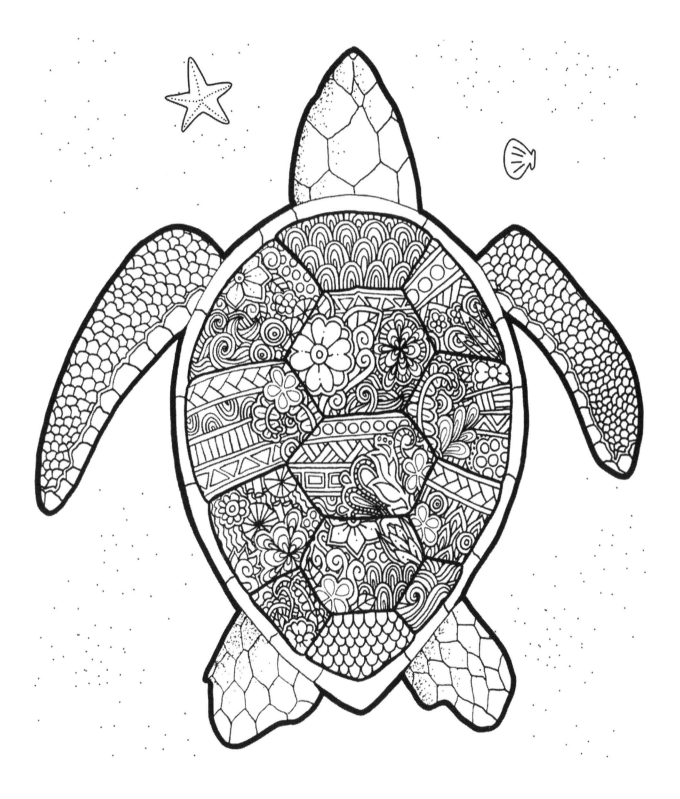

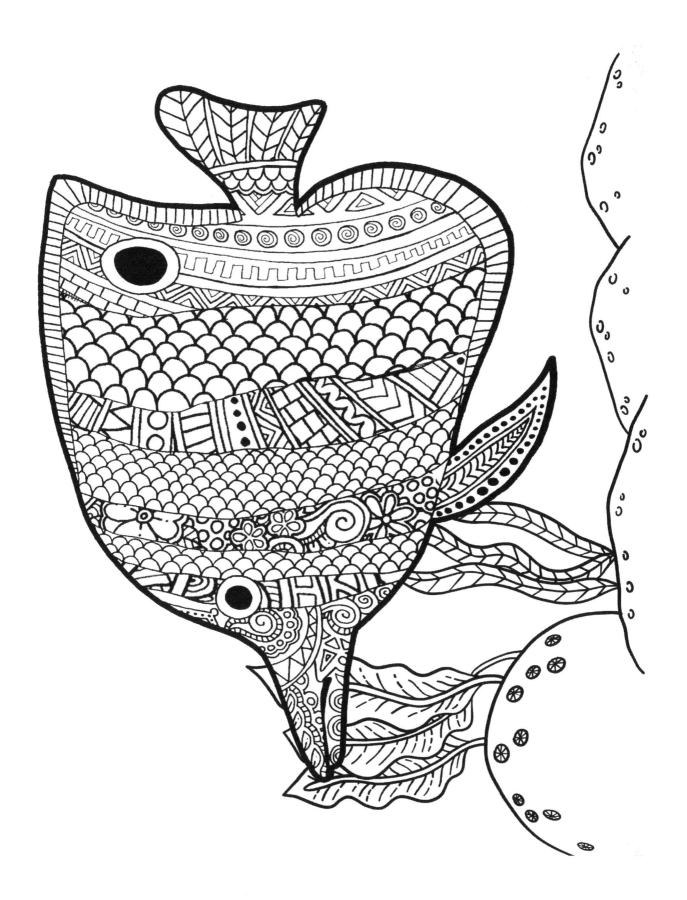

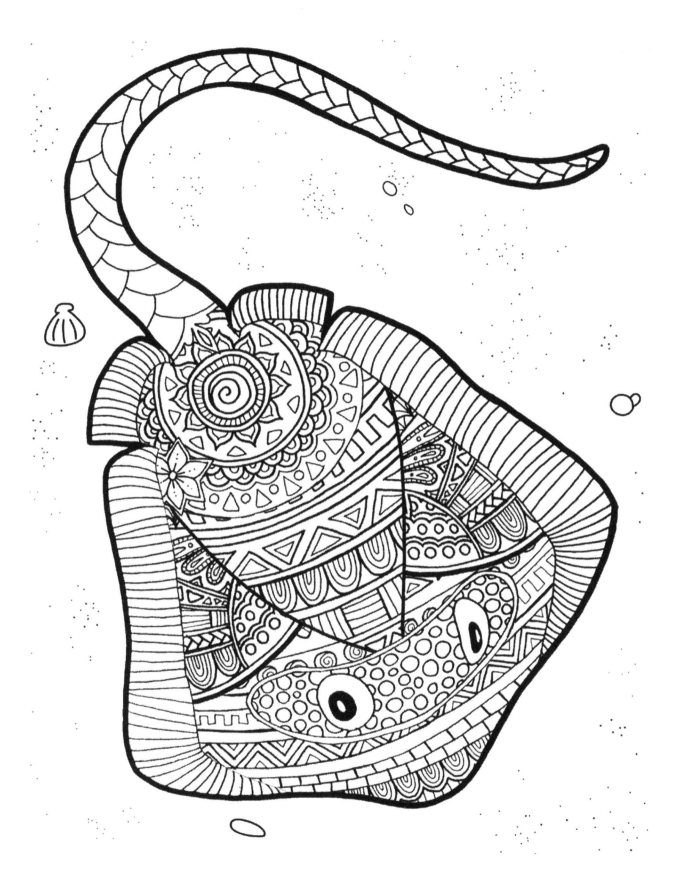

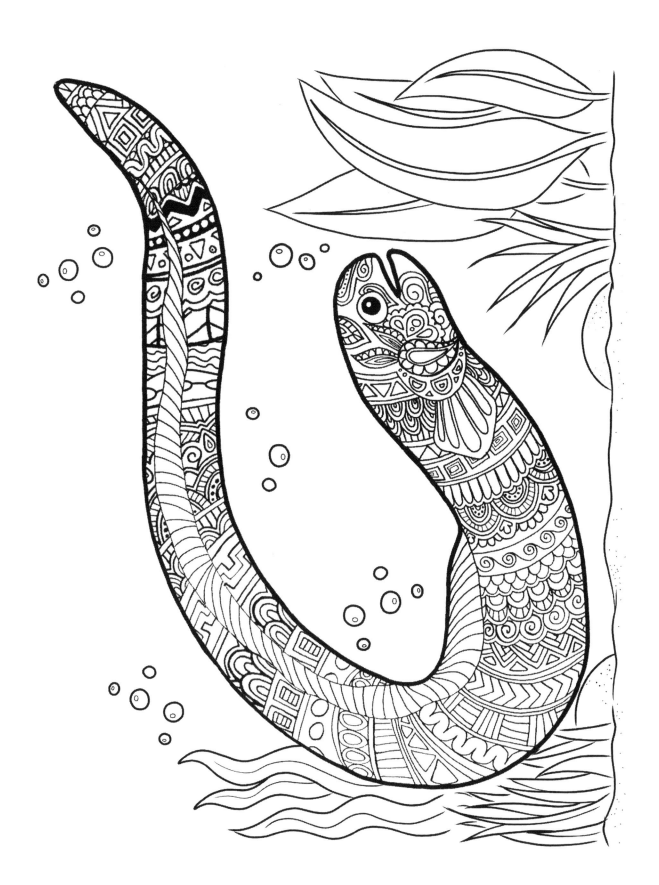

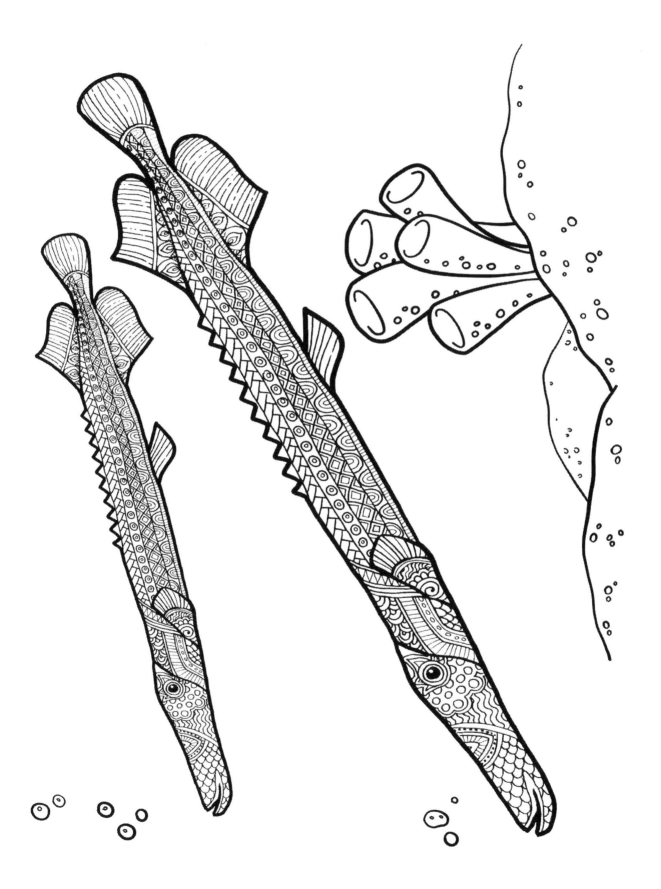

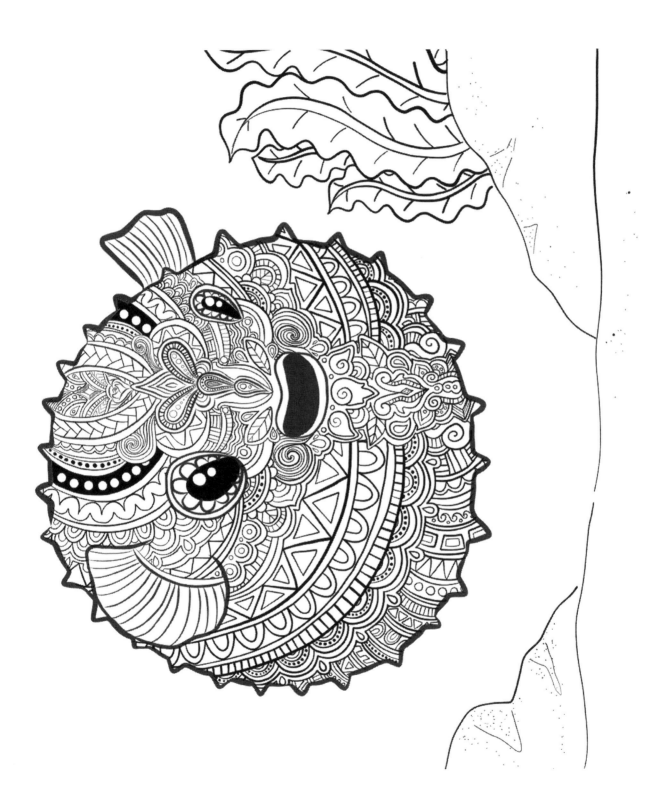

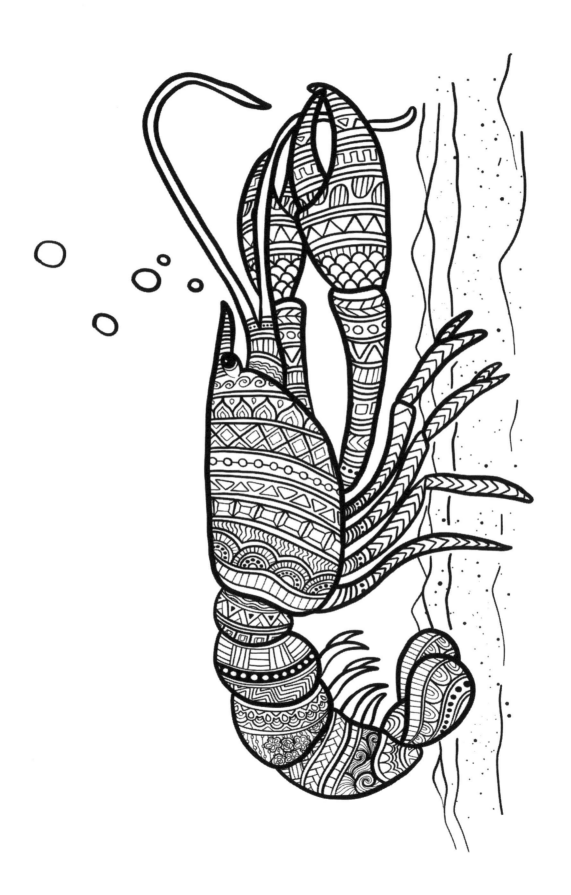

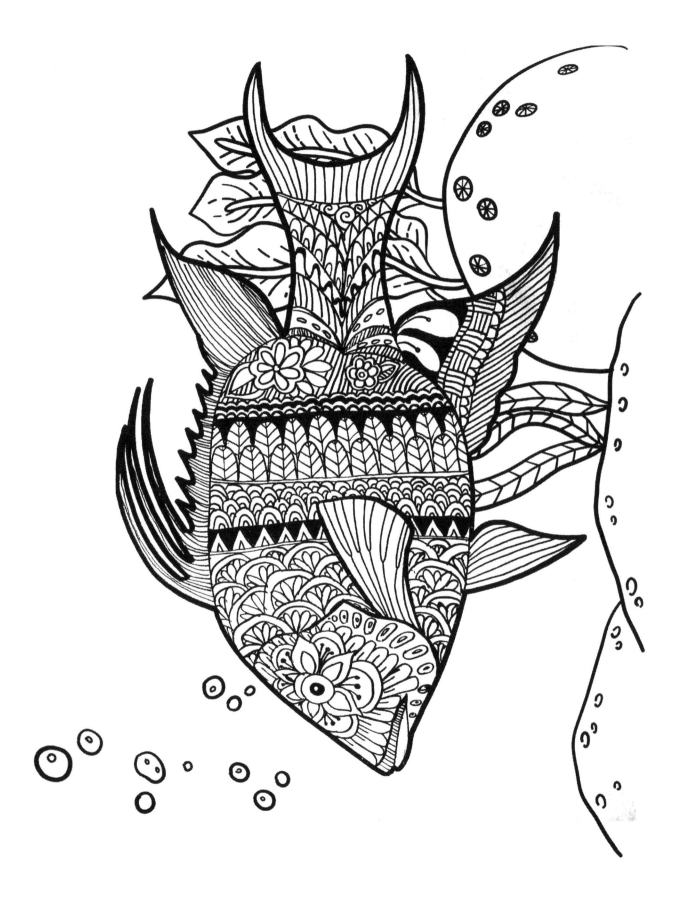

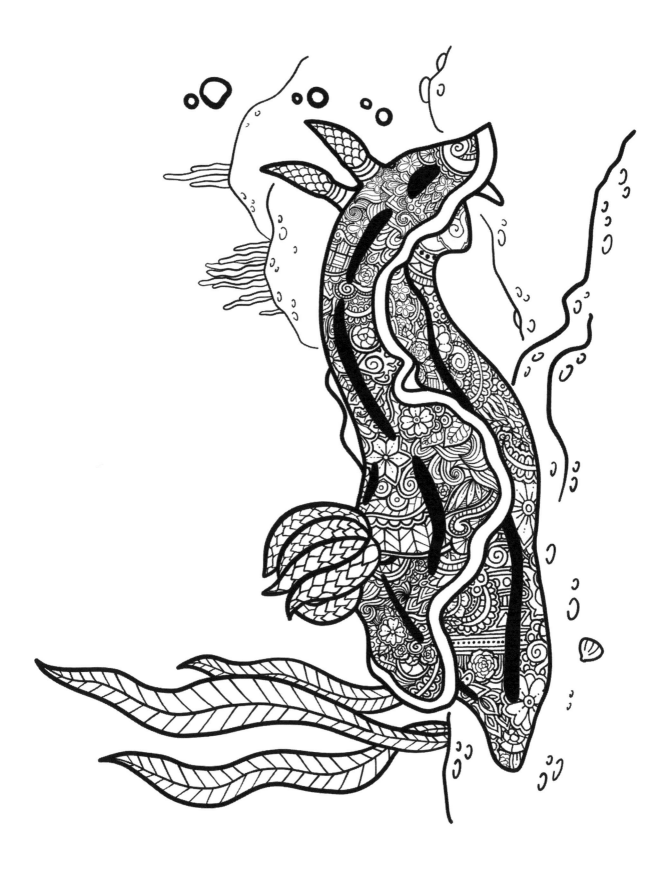

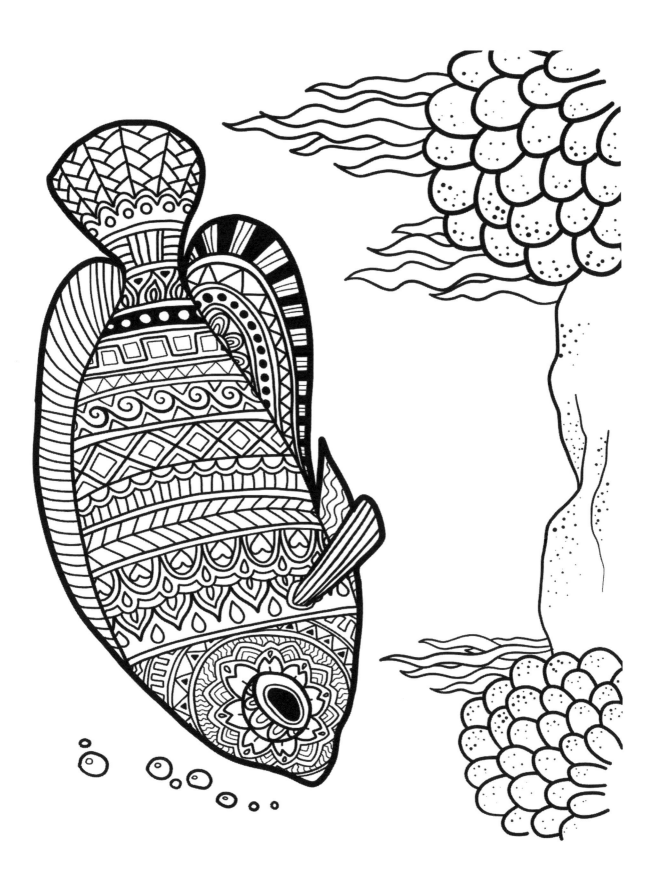

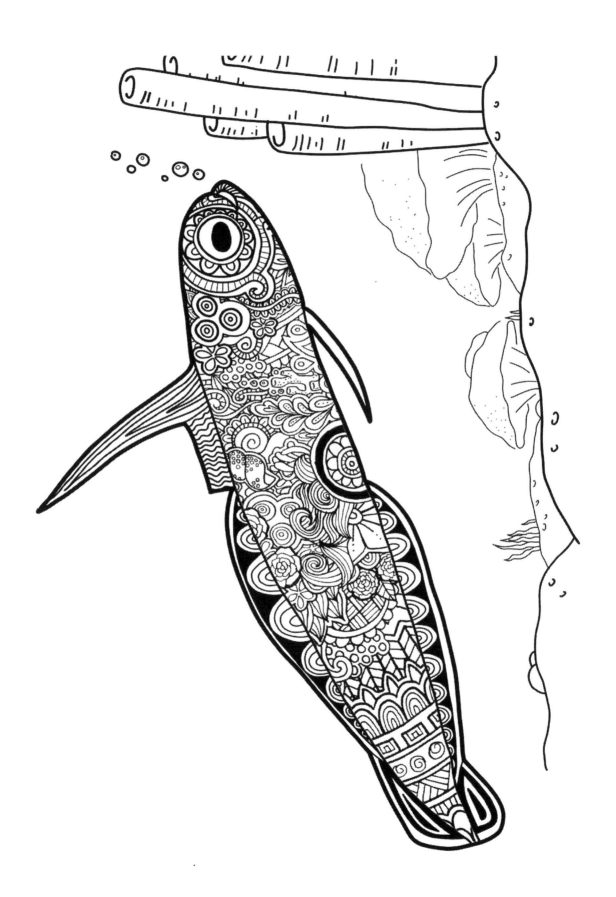

BONUS IMAGE TIME

To guarantee the satisfaction of our customers neither expenses nor efforts were avoided. We've gone the extra mile and included 7 Bonus Images, one each of our other 6 books. The style of the drawings may be a little bit different than the ones You may already have colored in this book. This ensures variety and will boost Your creativity even more. For more information about our other books, please see the last page of this book. We really hope that You will like them and have much fun coloring them.

AMAZING ANIMALS - FOR RELAXATION, MEDITATION, STRESS RELIEF, CALM
AND HEALING

AWESOME PHILIPPINES RELAX THERAPY - A MAGIC AND MINDFUL TRAVEL
ADVENTURE

AWESOME TESSELLATIONS FOR RELAXATION AND AGAINST STRESS

MAGIC FAIRY TALES AND AWESOME FANTASY CREATURES

MAGIC MERRY CHRISTMAS AND AMAZING WINTER FANTASIES

RELAX AND CALM - FOR RELAXATION, MEDITATION, STRESS RELIEF,
INSPIRATIONAL MINDFULNESS AND HEALING

CHINESE DRAGONS AND ASIAN LUCKY CHARMS

10 Lucky Compliments To Reduce Stress For Others

You probably have experienced receiving compliments from your friends, boss, and any other people. Have you noticed how this simple words have changed your mood, make you happier and less stressed? The same feeling will be received by others if you give those compliments, especially genuine ones. Compliments can be of great value particularly for individuals who are highly stressed out in life, or just for those who are having a bad day.

There are lots of stressors in our everyday busy lives, from arguments with the family, too much work, traffic, and any other triggers. Feeling stressed out may seem to be just normal, but people must be aware of its effect both on our health and in our daily function. Stressed-out individuals often need comforting words from their peers, or even from strangers.

Even though you really don't know what that person is exactly going through, you can lift up their mood through saying anything nice to them, nevertheless, it doesn't mean you have to lie. Only the simple sincere and genuine compliments can make their day. Here is some of what you can try:

1) **You always do a great job!**
   Everyone wants to feel that their efforts are valued. Through this simple compliment (make sure to say it in proper timing, and in genuine way), your co-workers, or even your little kids can feel that you appreciate what they do. Even though others may see it as not enough, if you have seen someone have place great amount of effort in everything she/he does, there is no reason to keep appreciation. If you are supposedly in the place of that person, more or less, you also want to hear nice thing from someone about your work.

2) **You are so strong and brave!**
   Stressful situations tend to make us weak at all points, saying this to a friend can help them be motivated, stand up, and get going. There are stressful days which we are too tried to continue or finish what we are doing. Through making others feel they are strong and brave, you are more likely enticing that strength, so they will have that notion to themselves "I am strong, I know I can do it!"

3) **You are brilliant!**

Stress often makes us intellectually tired, running out of ideas to solve a specific problem or situation. This compliment will more likely encourage your colleague to think of solutions to combat stressful situations. It's also like you trust their abilities and skills.

4) **You really look wonderful today!**

Who don't want to be praised by their physical appearance? Or simply get compliments for their outfit for the day (this compliment goes great for women)? Through simply saying you like her shoes can already lift up their mood.

5) **You're smile is contagious!**

Well, it's always a fact! Have you ever noticed yourself also smile when someone else does? Saying their smile is contagious can motivate them to wear their beautiful smile for the rest of their day. Smiling lift up moods and reduces stress even just a little bit of it.

6) **I am just too lucky to have your presence here!**

Make them feel their existence matters (although it really does, saying it will prove it further). Everybody simply wants belonging, to their peers, to their families, to their friends and any other circles. It is like saying indirectly to that person that he or she matters and you appreciate their presence.

7) **Our team is better because you are in it!**

It doesn't just lift up others mood, reduces stress but also boost self-esteem. It is just like saying "We are lucky to have you in our team".

8) **You are so authentic and real!**

Many people just play a role and don't be themselves in their lives. If you appreciate somebody for being authentic, he surely will appreciate you.

9) **You are one of a kind. You can always find the silver lining in everything!**

In every problem or stressful situation, there will always be something good that lies behind. You just need to be open-minded enough to find the good thing in the midst of the dark. Through saying this, you are more likely to open someone's eyes for the good things and focus on the positive rather than stressing each self to the problems.

10) Everyone sometimes get knocked down, only individuals like you stand up and get going!

This is just like saying "You are not the type of person who easily gives up".

If you are given an opportunity to say something nice to someone, never hesitate to say it, you don't know how much that person needs that. Make always sure to just say the compliments that are genuine and honest. An honest compliment weight more than piles of insincere ones.

Never underestimate the value and power of compliments in fighting stress. We are now living in a fast-pace and demanding environment where people seemed to focus only on one's self. Humans, in turn, tend to be highly stressed-out and tense. With lots of concern and responsibilities, majority of us wanted to scream "I can't handle these things anymore!" while our mind is searching in depth to find solutions and ways of how to handle this overwhelming things. We tend to be all tired, and down. Which in turn, can negatively impact both our daily living and our health.

Though you have your own problems and stressful days, don't forget to offer care to others (in simple way of providing compliments). Being generous enough to say uplifting words will not just soothe their souls, but also yours. It's just like you receive what you give.

Giving compliments, however, isn't a simple and easy thing for some. For some it takes guts. But why would you be scared on sharing all those good thoughts that keep on running on your mind? Try saying those great and wonderful thoughts you kept inside, and witness its great power. Nice words at a time can gradually ease peoples stress and even change the world.

MORE BONUS DESIGNS

For all subscribers of our Newsletter we give away another 10(!) FREE Bonus Relaxing Designs. They are beautiful, relaxing and with Your help they will become a true masterpiece.

Get them here:

http://relaxation4.me/bonus-relaxing-designs

"Like" This Book?
Your Facebook Friends Will Too

Do them a favor:

Share to Facebook:
www.relaxation4.me/share

Feedback

We Need Your Help! Please take a moment to rate this book on amazon. It will help us continue to make great books for You. If You love this book, please review it! :)

We love all our customers and give our best to provide the most value for the paper. In a passionate way of constant reach for perfection we would love to hear from You. Tell us Your opinion and wishes.

info@relaxation4.me

Thank You :)

Our Awesome Books

All our books include plenty of great illustrations which will benefit You with weeks of mind relaxation, creativity boosts and coloring fun. Additional to the many beautiful illustrations You will find 10 tips/advices for a more enriched life and 10 inspirational positive messages.
Check them out at www.amazon.com or visit us at www.relaxation4.me

★ MAGIC FAIRY TALES AND AWESOME FANTASY CREATURES

A magic coloring book full of cute mythical creatures like fairies, mermaids, demons and monsters. If you dreamed of being Alice in Wonderland this is the book of your choice.

Includes: 10 Magic Sleep Better Techniques

★ RELAX AND CALM - FOR RELAXATION, MEDITATION, STRESS RELIEF, INSPIRATIONAL MINDFULNESS AND HEALING

Are you looking for a way to feel relaxed and calm? Every single one of our coloring books will help you feeling these emotions. But this one with its lovely motives is hiding a treasure. Is it going to become your treasure?

Includes: 10 Health Boosting Superfoods Suggestions

★ AMAZING ANIMALS FOR RELAXATION, MEDITATION, STRESS RELIEF, CALM AND HEALING

The most famous creatures of the whole world, all featured in this book.
Beside many more you will find a cute baby owl, a penguin family and a nut eating squirrel. We love animals!

Includes: 10 Beautiful Relaxing Sound Suggestions

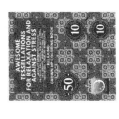

★ AWESOME TESSELLATION FOR RELAXATION AND AGAINST STRESS

Geometric shapes don't have to be associated with math class. In this book your left brain will meet your right brain and will be connected in a wonderful creative way.

Includes: 10 Effective Stress Reducing Techniques

★ AWESOME PHILIPPINES RELAX THERAPY - A MAGIC AND MINDFUL TRAVEL ADVENTURE

The Philippines are full of amazing and beautiful sceneries. You will find landscapes and cultural goods to color wich will let you develop a desire of travelling to the Philippines. This wonderful coloring book was illustrated by artists with disabilities and supports them.

Includes: 10 Strees Free Secrets

★ MAGIC MERRY CHRISTMAS AND AMAZING WINTER FANTASIES

Why just waiting for Christmas to recive a gift from Santa Clause, when you can make yourself a gift today? Decorations, presents, snowmen and even Santa Clause. Everything that is charming about Chritsmas and winter you will find in this book.

Includes: 10 Charming Relationship Advices

★ CHINESE DRAGONS AND ASIAN LUCKY CHARMS

If You thought coloring illustrations is a great hobby because it relaxes Your mind and boosts Your creativity, You are totally right. But what if coloring also attracts luck to Your life? With this coloring book You can try it out. 50 awesome illustrations full of luck. Be Your lucks' own architect.

Includes: 10 Ways To Attract Good Luck

Thank You!

64451668R00064

Made in the USA
San Bernardino, CA
22 December 2017